pour apprendre à dessiner en s'amusant !

Animaux et nature
Les animaux du Grand Nord ● Les animaux d'Afrique ● Les animaux de la forêt ●
Les animaux de la maison ● Les animaux de la ferme ● Les animaux du monde ● La mer ●
La campagne ● La montagne ● Le bord de l'eau ● Les dinosaures ● Les oiseaux du monde ●
Les chiens ● Chevaux et poneys ● Les chats ● Les fleurs ● Les dragons ● Les bébés animaux ●
Le poney-club ●

Personnages
Les contes ● Le cirque ● La famille ● L'école ● Les monstres ● Les sports ●
La crèche de Noël ● Noël ● Les princesses ● Les fées ● La danse ●

Métiers
Les pompiers ● Chez le vétérinaire ●

Histoire
L'Égypte ● Chevaliers et châteaux forts ● Les Gaulois ● La préhistoire ● Les pirates ●

Moyens de transport
Les voitures et les motos ● Les camions ● Les avions ● Les bateaux ●
Les trains ● Les engins de chantier ●

Techniques
Dessiner les belles lettres ● Peindre à la gouache ● Dessiner au compas ●
Dessiner au crayon de couleur ● Découper ●

Hors-série
Mes animaux préférés de A à Z ● Mes personnages préférés de A à Z ●
L'Histoire de France ●

Les compilations
La nature ● Les animaux lointains ● Peindre et dessiner ● Un monde magique ●
Créer de jolis décors ● La vie quotidienne ● Les moyens de transport ●
Les princesses et les chevaliers ●

Philippe Legendre

J'APPRENDS À DESSINER

les dinosaures

FLEURUS

www.fleuruseditions.com

À l'attention des parents et des enseignants

Tous les enfants savent dessiner un rond, un carré, un triangle…
Alors, ils peuvent aussi dessiner un stégosaure, un tricératops et un diplodocus.
Notre méthode est facile et amusante. Elle apporte à l'enfant une technique
et un vocabulaire des formes dont se sert tout dessinateur.
La construction du dessin se fait par l'association de formes géométriques
créant un ensemble de volumes/surfaces. Il suffit ensuite, par une ligne droite,
courbe ou brisée, de donner son caractère définitif à l'esquisse.
En quelques coups de crayon un motif apparaît,
un peu de couleur et voici réalisée une belle illustration.
Cette méthode propose un apprentissage de la technique
et une première approche de la composition, des proportions, du volume,
de la ligne. Sa simplicité en fait une méthode où le plaisir
de dessiner reste au premier plan.

PHILIPPE LEGENDRE
Peintre-graveur et illustrateur, Philippe Legendre anime
aussi un atelier de peinture pour les enfants de 6 à 14 ans.
Intervenant souvent en milieu scolaire, il a développé
cette méthode pour que tous les enfants puissent
accéder à l'art du dessin.

Quelques conseils

Chaque dessin est fait à partir d'un petit nombre de formes géométriques qui sont indiquées en haut de la page.
C'est ce qu'on appelle le vocabulaire de formes.
Il peut te servir à t'exercer avant de commencer le dessin.

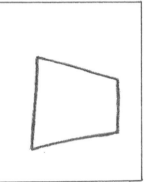

1. Fais l'esquisse du dessin au crayon et à main levée. Attention, pas de règle ni de compas !

2. Les pointillés indiquent les traits de construction qui doivent être gommés.

3. Une fois ton dessin terminé, colorie-le. Si tu veux, repasse en noir le trait de crayon.

Et maintenant, à toi de jouer !

L'iguanodon...

n'était pas méchant.

Il avait une centaine de dents...

mais ne mangeait que des feuilles.

L'iguanodon

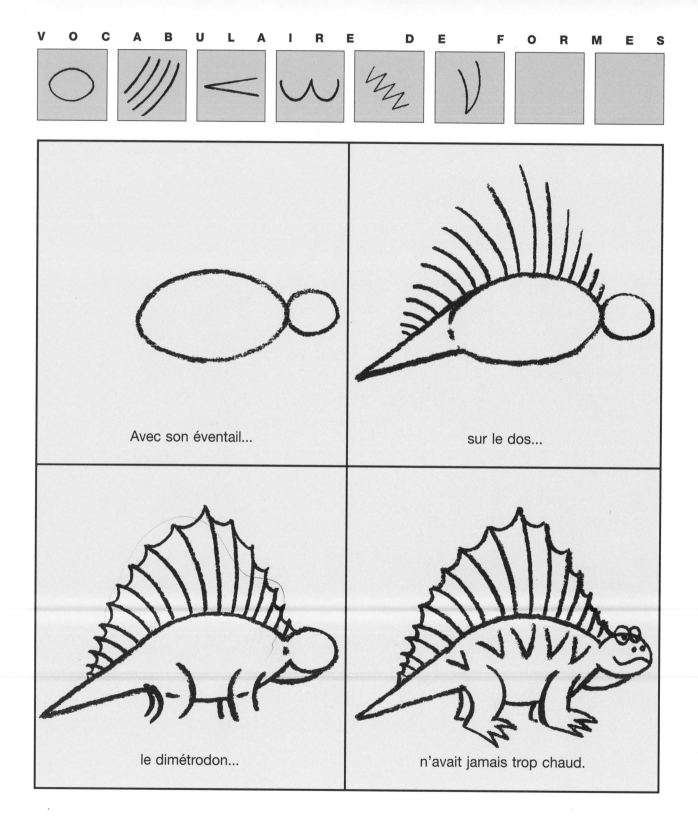

Avec son éventail...

sur le dos...

le dimétrodon...

n'avait jamais trop chaud.

Le dimétrodon

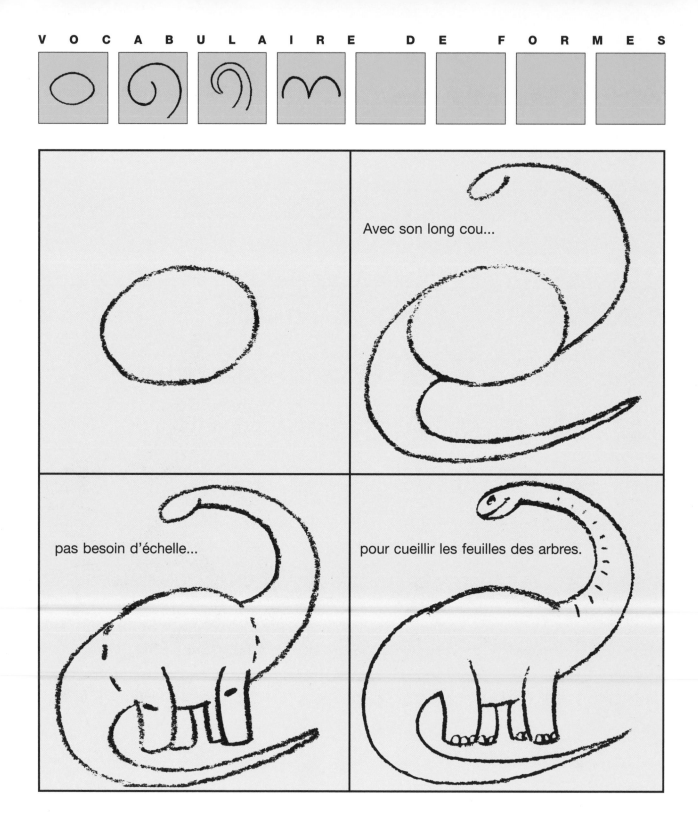

Avec son long cou...

pas besoin d'échelle...

pour cueillir les feuilles des arbres.

Le diplodocus

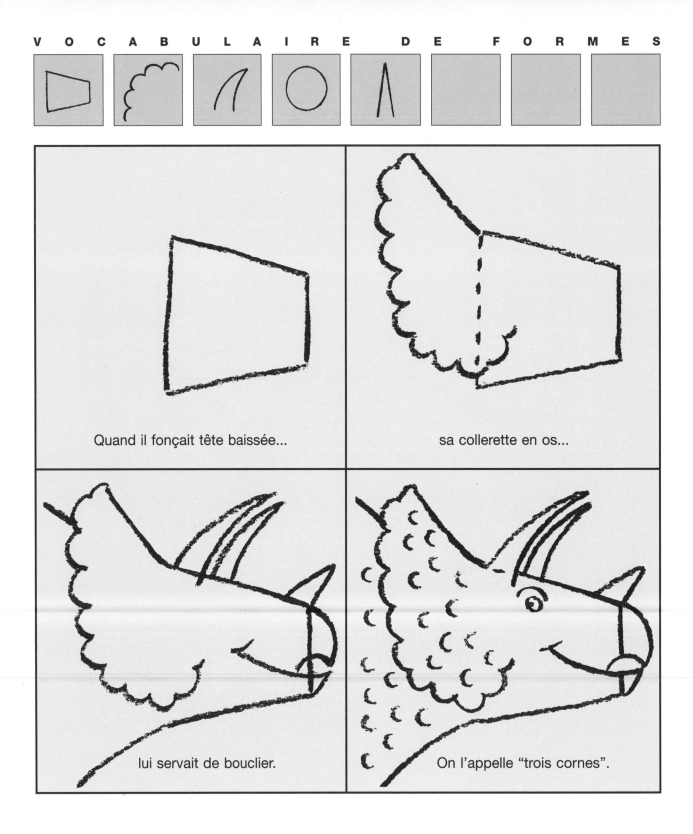

Quand il fonçait tête baissée...

sa collerette en os...

lui servait de bouclier.

On l'appelle "trois cornes".

Le tricératops

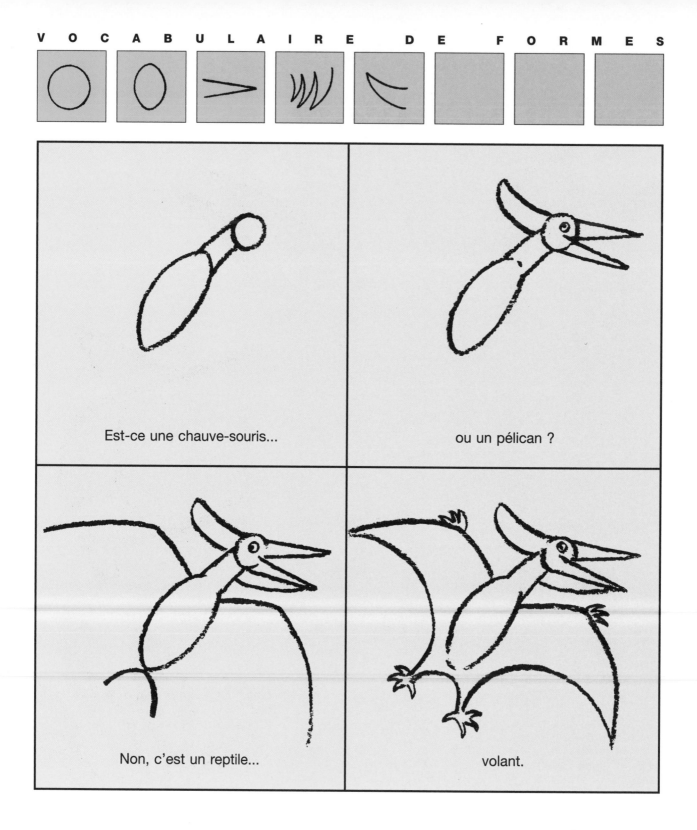

Est-ce une chauve-souris...

ou un pélican ?

Non, c'est un reptile...

volant.

Le ptéranodon

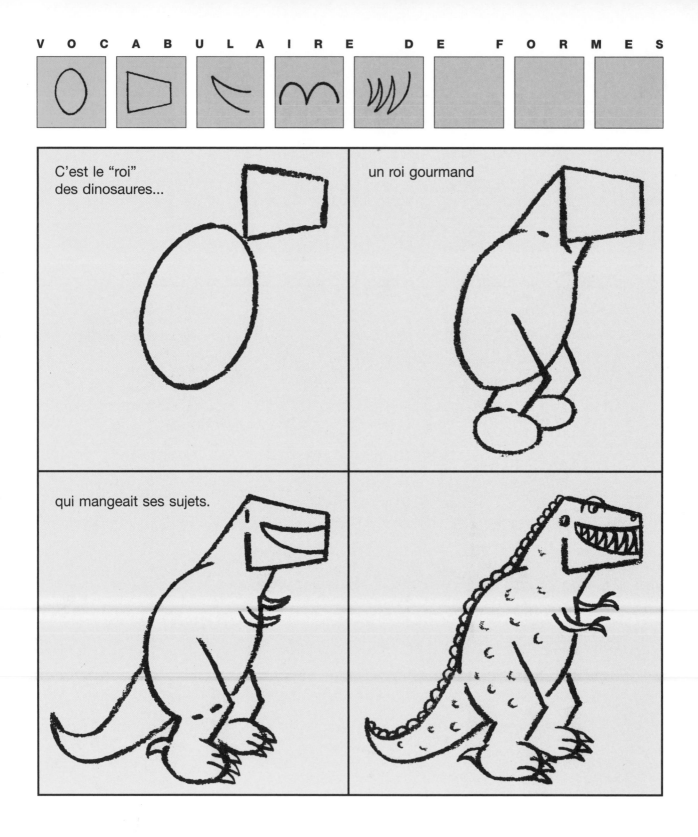

C'est le "roi"
des dinosaures...

un roi gourmand

qui mangeait ses sujets.

Le tyrannosaure rex

Son nom veut dire...

"le reptile avec un toit".

Mais a-t-il mis les tuiles...

dans le bon sens ?

Le stégosaure

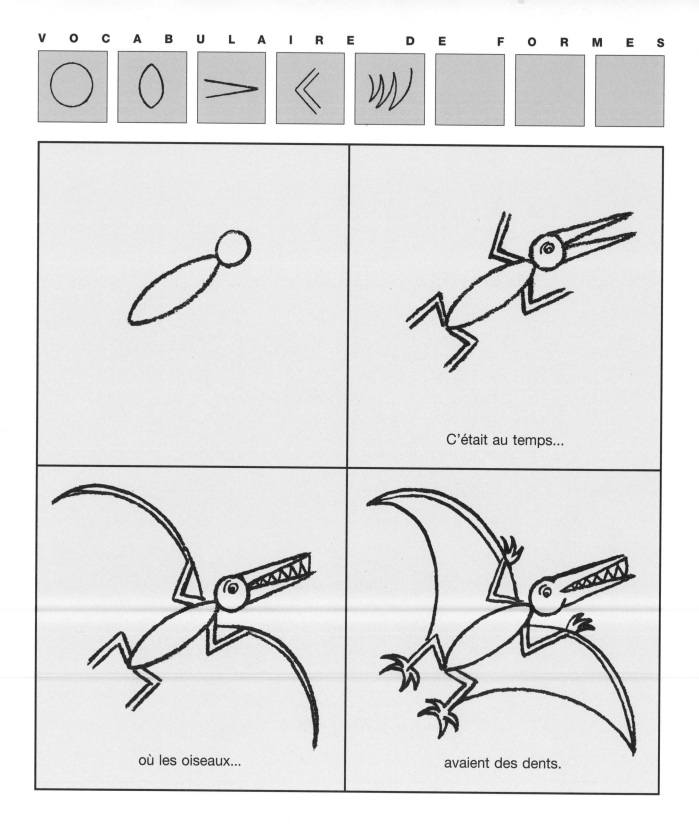

C'était au temps...

où les oiseaux...

avaient des dents.

Le ptérodactyle

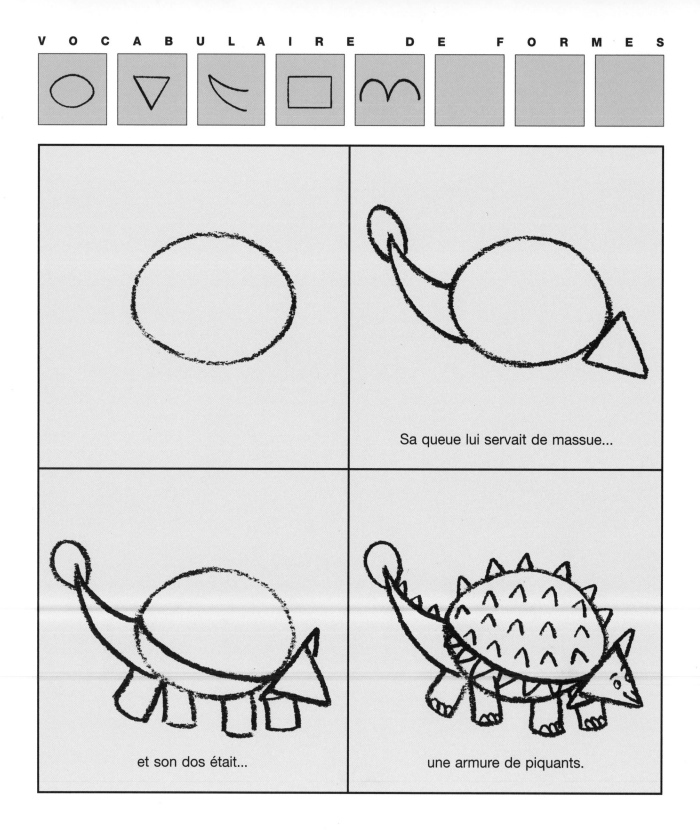

Sa queue lui servait de massue...

et son dos était...

une armure de piquants.

L'ankylosaure

Tous ces animaux ont mystérieusement disparu il y a 65 millions d'années. Mais tu peux les faire revivre en les dessinant.
Sais-tu quel est l'animal le plus ancien ?

Loi n°49-956 du 16 juillet 1949 sur les publications destinées à la jeunesse.

Direction éditoriale : Christophe Savouré
Direction artistique : Armelle Riva
Couverture : Armelle Riva
Conception graphique de la collection : Isabelle Bochot

© 2007 Fleurus Éditions (1re édition 1996)
15/27 rue Moussorgski, 75018 Paris
Dépôt légal : mai 2007
ISBN : 978-2-215-09407-4
ISSN : 1257-9629
6e édition - N° P12101

Imprimé en Slovénie par PPF-France en juillet 2012

WE DEDICATE THIS BOOK TO THE SWEET
INNOCENCE LIVING IN EACH OF OUR HEARTS,
FROM WHICH, THE JOY OF GIVING
SPONTANEOUSLY FLOWS.

ANDREW'S WISH

WRITTEN BY JASON M. LEEN & JAN A. KLYCE

ILLUSTRATED BY GARY LUND

J & J PUBLISHING

PETALUMA, CALIFORNIA

J&J
PUBLISHING

Enjoy J.
2019
Jan A. Klyce

Now, I know you've heard the story about Rudolf,
of his red nose and all,
but there's someone just as important
who never heard Santa's call.

He was sleeping, oh so soundly
in his heated waterbed
while visions of roasted apples
danced merrily 'round his head.

His given name was Andrew,
but he didn't like that at all;
in fact, when the others called, "Andrew,"
he would not answer their call.

For when he was just a young reindeer,
his antlers not yet fully grown,
the others giggled and laughed at his name,
leaving Andrew to feel so alone.

This is why he needed a clock,
to awaken him from his dreams,
for he would not respond to his name,
no matter how loud it was screamed!

So on that fateful night,
while Rudolf guided the sleigh,
Andrew was sleeping, so soundly,
never knowing his clock was delayed.

When the alarm finally woke him,
he dressed in his wintry best,
but as he called out for the others,
he discovered that he'd overslept.

At first he was so disappointed,
all because his clock didn't chime!
Then he saw something very important,
a box full of gifts left behind.

Oh, how could this have happened!
He could not believe his eyes.
Andrew thought of the children
with no Christmas morning surprise.

Not stopping to think of himself,
Andrew knew just what to do.
He would ask the King of the Elves
to help make his wish come true.

He would ask the elven elders
to do what they always do best.
He would ask them to use their magic.
Then he would do the rest!

Balancing the box with care,
to the Elven Kingdom he went.
He suddently was was much more daring
then he could have ever dreamt.

Passing quickly through Santa's village,
all was silent and, oh so still.
He set his course and kept his sight
on the kingdom's light beyond the hills.

Climbing up and down the winding path
all covered in a blanket of white,
step by step through the sparkling snow,
he journeyed deep into the night.

Under a glittering star-filled sky,
Andrew arrived at the elven door.
He told the king of his heart's desire,
setting the gifts on the wooden floor.

At first the king sat silently.
A stillness filled the air.
He bowed his head and closed his eyes
as though he didn't care.

Then suddenly, the king stood up,
refreshed and renewed.
With a smile, he turned to the elves;
Andrew's wish had been approved.

Quickly, the elves gathered 'round him,
each moving without delay
as Andrew wished his magic wish
that the gifts would find their way.

There were flutes of the finest silver,
tea sets made for a queen,
trains that somehow seemed alive,
ready to take us to the land of our dreams.

There were puzzles that defied solution,
dancing bears who never tired.
There were mysteries and surprises,
all waiting to be admired.

In a twinkling, the gifts were gone,
transported through time and space,
directed to their exact destination
and destined to arrive at that place.

All the elves cheered for Andrew,
expressing their love so heartfelt.
For being so good and doing all that he could,
they made him an honorary elf!

Andrew was so happy
all the gifts had found their way
that at first he did not notice,
the gift he'd received that day.

Then as the elves all shouted, "Andrew,"
he smiled as he realized
for the very first time he loved his name,
and he laughed until he cried.

For now as his name was called,
he heard a magical ring,
a wonderful and glorious sound
that made his big heart sing.

Andrew had never expected,
not once had it entered his mind,
that by wanting to give, he would receive
this gift for being so kind.

Knowing their work was complete,
the elves gathered 'round him so close.
Now you know why Andrew's wish
is as important as Rudolf's nose!

First edition published by

J & J PUBLISHING
PO Box 751351, Petaluma, CA 94975-1351
Tel: 707-762-1566 . Fax: 707-762-1466
info@jandj-publishing.com
www.jandj-publishing.com

Publication Data

Leen, Jason M., Klyce, Jan A., 2009
Andrew's Wish - written by Jason M. Leen and Jan A. Klyce; Illustrated by Gary Lund

Summary: A reindeer named Andrew who oversleeps on Christmas Eve finds a box
of gifts Santa left behind. His heartfelt wish for the gifts to find their way to the children
by Christmas morning leads him on a heroic journey to the Elven Kingdom, where, with
the magical powers of the Elven King, Andrew's wish is granted along with another
very wonderful and unexpected surprise.

ISBN - 13: 978-0-9824998-0-1: $15.95

[1. Christmas-Fiction. 2. Stories in rhyme. 3. Reindeer-Fiction 4. Elf kingdom-Fiction
5. Magic-Fiction 6. Joy of giving-Fiction] 1. Title

Library of Congress Control Number: 2009931293

Published in the United States of America
Printed by Tien Wah Press in Singapore
Book layout, design and art direction by Jan Klyce

WITH SPECIAL THANKS TO:

Kelsey Grammer for his charming, joy-filled and heartfelt audio recording that accompanies this book. As we hear him read the verses, Kelsey's qualities of kindness and compassion are ever present in this story of Andrew's Wish. Besides being known for his internationally loved and long-running character, Dr. Frasier Crane, Kelsey, a Shakespearean-trained actor, singer, and successful producer, is a rare gem, who continues to delight audiences with his live stage, film and television performances.

Gary Lund for all his care and devotion in bringing Andrew's world to life through his amazing, sweet, beautiful, and often humorous illustrations. Gary's artistic talent in magazine, children's and non-fiction book illustrations, film animation, including storyboard, character, and background design, is equaled by his loving, kind, and humble personality. He has been a total delight to work with on this project.

Maria Christina Paleari, whose love and support made it possible to bring this special story into a finished book that can now be shared with children everywhere, and enjoyed by all the young at heart.

Christine George for all her technical, artistic, and emotional support. Christine is a very talented equine fine artist, photographer, and graphic designer, who also teaches graphic design at the Academy of Art University in San Francisco, California.

Bruce Greenspan for his excellent sound recording and editing services for the audio CD of Andrew's Wish. Bruce works with Planet Grande Pictures in Malibu, California.

Dear Parent:
Your child's love of reading starts here!

Every child learns to read in a different way and at his or her own speed. Some go back and forth between reading levels and read favorite books again and again. Others read through each level in order. You can help your young reader improve and become more confident by encouraging his or her own interests and abilities. From books your child reads with you to the first books he or she reads alone, there are I Can Read Books for every stage of reading:

SHARED READING
Basic language, word repetition, and whimsical illustrations, ideal for sharing with your emergent reader

BEGINNING READING
Short sentences, familiar words, and simple concepts for children eager to read on their own

READING WITH HELP
Engaging stories, longer sentences, and language play for developing readers

READING ALONE
Complex plots, challenging vocabulary, and high-interest topics for the independent reader

ADVANCED READING
Short paragraphs, chapters, and exciting themes for the perfect bridge to chapter books

I Can Read Books have introduced children to the joy of reading since 1957. Featuring award-winning authors and illustrators and a fabulous cast of beloved characters, I Can Read Books set the standard for beginning readers.

A lifetime of discovery begins with the magical words "I Can Read!"

Visit www.icanread.com for information
on enriching your child's reading experience.

For Adele Hanna—with love.

This 2011 edition was created exclusively for Sandy Creek by arrangement with HarperCollins Publishers.

HarperCollins Publishers® and I Can Read Book® are registered trademarks.
No More Monsters for Me! Text copyright © 1981 by Margaret Parish Illustrations copyright © 1981 by Marc Simont
www.icanread.com

Sandy Creek
387 Park Avenue South
New York, NY 10016

ISBN 978-1-4351-3709-7

Manufactured in China
Manufactured April 2012
Lot 12 13 14 15 SCP 10 9 8 7 6 5 4 3 2

An I Can Read!™
Picture Book

No More Monsters for Me!

by Peggy Parish

pictures by Marc Simont

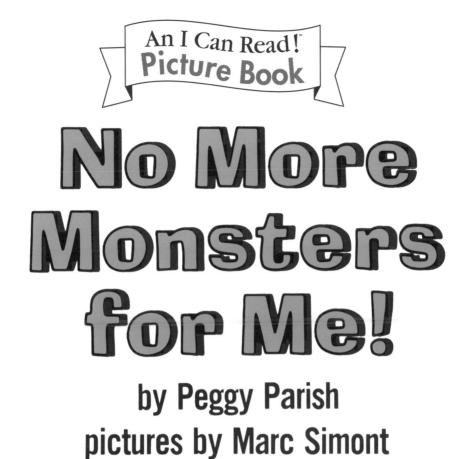

Sandy Creek
NEW YORK

"Not even a tadpole,

Minneapolis Simpkin,"

yelled Mom.

"And I mean it!"

"Okay, okay,"

I yelled back.

5

Mom and I always yell a lot.

But this time,

she was really mad.

And so was I.

I stamped out of the house.

I did not care

what Mom said.

I was going to have a pet.

I would take a long walk

and think about this.

So I walked

down the road.

Suddenly I heard

a funny noise.

The noise came

from the bushes.

I stopped and listened.

"Something is crying,
Minneapolis Simpkin,"
I said to myself.
"I will find out

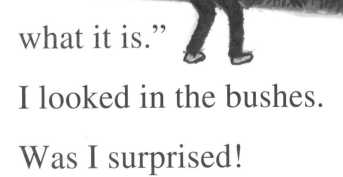

what it is."

I looked in the bushes.

Was I surprised!

9

"Wow! A baby monster!"

I yelled.

I looked at the monster.

It looked at me.

Then it ran to me.

I put my arms around it.

"Don't cry," I said.

"Minneapolis Simpkin

will help you."

The monster stopped crying.

We stood there

hugging each other.

"A monster for a pet?"

I asked.

Mom never said no

to a monster.

But I never asked her that.

Will she say yes?

I needed time

to think about this.

But there was no time.

It started raining.

The monster did not like it.

It started bawling.

And I do mean bawling!

"Okay, okay," I said.

I grabbed the monster.

I ran home with it.

Mom was in the kitchen.

She did not see me.

But she heard me.

"Are you wet?" she asked.

"Yes," I said.

"Hurry and get dry,"

she said.

"Supper is about ready."

I ran to my room.

"So far, so good,"

I said to myself.

"But what now,

Minneapolis Simpkin?"

I shook my head.

I did not know.

"Minn," yelled Mom,

"supper is ready."

"Coming," I yelled back.

I started to go down.

The monster came, too.

"No," I said.

"You can't come."

I put the monster

in my closet.

It started bawling again.

What was I going to do?

I looked all around.

"My teddy bear!" I said.

I got the teddy bear.

"Here," I said.

The monster grabbed the bear.

It stopped crying.

I ran down to supper.

Mom had made a good supper.

Then I thought of something.

Monsters have to eat, too.

"Mom," I said,

"what do monsters eat?"

"Food, I guess," said Mom.

"But what kind?" I asked.

"Oh," said Mom.

"Is this a new game?"

19

Mom loves to play games.

So I said, "Yes."

"Let me think," said Mom.

"What *do* monsters eat?"

I was glad to let her think,

because I saw something.

I saw the monster.

"I will be right back,"

I yelled.

"I have to get something."

I had to get something, all right.

I had to get the monster hidden.

I grabbed the monster.

I took it to the basement.

The monster started crying again.

"Quiet!" I said.

"If Mom hears you,

we are in for it."

I grabbed an apple.

"Here," I said.

The monster took the apple.

It stopped crying.

I grabbed another apple.

I ran back to the table.

"Here, Mom," I said.

I gave the apple to her.

"What is this for?"

she asked.

I didn't know what to say.

But I had to say something.

"Because I love you," I said.

Mom laughed.

"Minneapolis Simpkin," she said,

"I love you, too."

Then Mom said, "Pickles!"

"Pickles?" I said.

"Of course," said Mom.

"Monsters love pickles."

"I didn't know that," I said.

Then I asked,

"Do you know where monsters live?"

"Yes," said Mom.

"They live in caves.

Deep dark caves."

"Gee, Mom," I said.

"You know a lot about monsters."

"I love monster stories,"

said Mom.

"I read lots of them."

Did Mom like real monsters, too?

I started to ask her.

But I didn't.

The basement door was opening.

"I will be right back, Mom,"

I yelled.

"Minneapolis Simpkin!"

yelled Mom.

"Can't you sit still?"

"Hic-cup, hic-cup!"

Oh, no!

The monster had hiccups.

"Now you have the hiccups,"

yelled Mom.

"I will get some water,"

I yelled back.

"HIC-CUP! HIC-CUP!"

I opened the basement door.

My eyes almost popped out.

"You grew!" I yelled.

"What did you say?"

asked Mom.

"Nothing," I said.

I pushed the monster

back into the basement.

It was awful.

The monster was huge.

It was lumpy.

"HIC-CUP! HIC-CUP!"

I got some water.

"Drink this," I said.

The monster drank the water.

The hiccups stopped.

"Minn," yelled Mom,

"please bring me

another apple."

"Okay," I yelled back.

But there were

no more apples.

Now I knew

why the monster was lumpy.

I grabbed a potato.

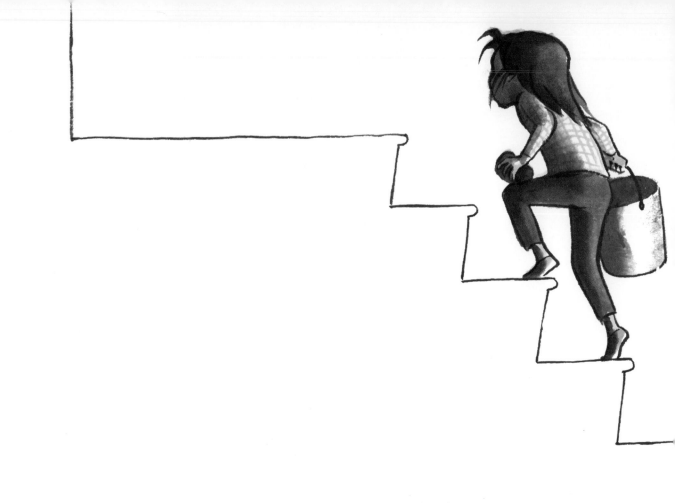

The monster

grabbed it from me.

I grabbed another one

and ran.

I locked the basement door.

"Here, Mom," I said.

"Minn, this is a potato,"
said Mom.

"I asked for an apple."

"Oh, sorry, Mom," I said.

"Minn," said Mom,

"why are you so jumpy?

Is something wrong?"

Something wrong?

Was it ever!

But maybe Mom could help.

So I said, "I am fine.

Tell me some more about monsters.

Where are those caves?"

"Up in the hills," said Mom.

"But don't bother

to look for one."

"Why not?" I asked.

"They are all hidden," she said.

"Only monsters can find them."

"Are you sure?" I asked.

"That is what

my mother told me,"

said Mom.

"I looked and I looked.

I never could find one."

I sure hoped Mom was right.

I had to get that monster home.

It was not a good pet.

Then it happened.

CRASH!

Mom jumped up.

"What was that?"

she asked.

Then she looked at me.

"Minn," she said,

"you were in the basement."

I nodded my head.

"Did you bring home

an animal?"

I nodded my head again.

"Minneapolis Simpkin!"

yelled Mom.

"I said NO PETS!"

"It is not a pet!"

I yelled back.

"Then what is it?"

yelled Mom.

I did not mean to.

I did not want to.

But I started bawling.

"It is a monster!"

I bawled.

I waited for

Mom to yell.

But she didn't.

"Oh, Minn," she said.

"You really need a pet,

don't you?"

"Yes," I bawled.

"But I want a kitten

or a puppy.

I don't want a monster."

"No," said Mom.

"A monster is not a good pet."

I stopped bawling.

"Now," said Mom,

"go and close that window."

"Window! What window?"

I asked.

"The basement window,"

said Mom.

"I must have left it open."

I just looked at her.

I still did not understand.

"Minneapolis Simpkin!"

said Mom.

"The wind is blowing hard.

It blew something over.

That is what made the noise.

Go close the window."

I went.

There was a window open.

The potato basket

was turned over.

The potatoes were all gone.

But the monster

was still there.

It was sleeping.

I looked at it.

How would I ever

get it out of the basement?

It was getting

bigger and bigger.

I went back to Mom.

"I closed the window,"

I said.

"The monster is there.

But it is sleeping."

"Okay, Minn, you win,"

said Mom.

"I was wrong.

I will make a deal.

You get rid of your monster,

and you can have

a real pet.

Deal?"

"Deal!" I cried.

That monster was no pet.

But it was real.

"Good," said Mom.

"I am going to take

a long bath.

You get rid of

your monster."

"Sure, Mom," I said.

I was not sure.

But I was sure

going to try.

I woke up the monster.

"Come on," I said.

"We are going."

The monster came.

52

It had to crawl

through the doors.

And I had to push

from behind.

But we made it.

I headed for the hills.

The monster followed.

The night was very dark.

I don't like the dark.

But I had to get

that monster home.

We got to the hills.

The monster looked at them.

It made happy noises.

"Is this your home?"

I asked.

The monster turned to me.

Suddenly

we were hugging each other.

Then the monster

ran up the hill.

I felt good.

The monster

had found its home.

"No more monsters for me,"

I said.

I ran all the way home.

Mom was yelling for me.

I went into the house.

"Minneapolis Simpkin!"
yelled Mom.

"Where have you been?"

"Getting rid of the monster,"
I yelled back.

"That is what

you told me to do."

I started to bawl again.

Mom looked at me

in a funny way.

She hugged me.

Then I knew.

I knew Mom didn't believe

that monster was real.

But Mom kept our deal.

We went to the pet shop.

Mom really surprised me.

She bought two kittens.

"Two!" I said.

"Sure," said Mom.

"One for you,

and one for me."

"Mom," I said,

"you are okay."

"And so are you, Minn,"

said Mom.

We each took a kitten.

And we went home.

AIRCRAFT CARRIERS
AT SEA

RICHARD AND LOUISE SPILSBURY

PowerKiDS
press

New York

Published in 2018 by **The Rosen Publishing Group, Inc.**
29 East 21st Street, New York, NY 10010

Cataloging-in-Publication

Names: Spilsbury, Richard. | Spilsbury, Louise.
Title: Aircraft carriers at sea / Richard and Louise Spilsbury.
Description: New York : PowerKids Press, 2018. | Series: Machines at sea | Includes index.
Identifiers: ISBN 9781499434507 (pbk.) | ISBN 9781499434453 (library bound) |
   ISBN 9781499434354 (6 pack)
Subjects: LCSH: Aircraft carriers--Juvenile literature.
Classification: LCC V874.S65 2018 | DDC 623.825'5--dc23

Copyright © 2018 by The Rosen Publishing Group, Inc.

Produced for Rosen by Calcium
Editors for Calcium: Sarah Eason and Jennifer Sanderson
Designers for Calcium: Paul Myerscough and Jennie Child
Picture researcher: Harriet McGregor

Photo Credits: Cover: Harry Andrew D. Gordon, U.S. Navy. Inside: Shutterstock: David Acosta
Allely 7, 13, Apiguide 31, Cowardlion 25, Everett Historical 9, Derek Gordon 10, 17, 22, Jason
and Bonnie Grower 21, 26, Vladislav Gurfinkel 14, Bastian Kienitz 18, Joyce Marrero 16,
RestonImages 8, SpaceKris 27, Jeff Whyte 6, 11; U.S. Navy: Petty Officer 3rd Class Anderson
W. Branch 5, Mass Communication Specialist 1st Class Denny Cantrell 28–29, DoD/Mass
Communication Specialist 3rd Class R.U. Kledzik 24, DoD/PH3 Bruce W. Moore 15, Mass
Communication Specialist 1st Class Sarah Murphy 19, 3rd Class Craig R. Spiering 23.

Manufactured in China
CPSIA Compliance Information: Batch BS17PK: For Further Information contact Rosen Publishing, New York, New York at 1-800-237-9932.

AIRCRAFT CARRIERS AT SEA

OATING
AIR BASES

a small air base, you see several aircraft, buildings in which to keep t, runways, a control tower to manage takeoffs and landings, and many nbers to keep everything running smoothly. When all of this is put on hip, you have an aircraft carrier.

r Basics

t carrier is a ship with a long, wide platform built on top, called a **flight** e flight deck is the runway, where aircraft land and take off. The tallest e carrier is called the **island**. It is part control tower for aircraft and part /hich is where the ship is controlled.

PEARL HARBOR

The devastating power of aircraft carriers was first demonstrated in World War II. In 1941, Japanese airplanes launched from aircraft carriers destroyed Pearl Harbor, the United States' naval harbor in Hawaii. Since this lethal coming of age, aircraft carriers have become major ships in many navies.

Why Carry Aircraft?

Aircraft can fly to and from air bases to places where they take part in military and other actions. However, small aircraft do not have a great range, or distance, and can operate only on their own fuel supply. Navies are usually on missions far from home, so they use air bases where aircraft can be refueled, maintained, and have their supply of missiles and ammunition refilled.

An aircraft carrier is a portable air base. It can travel near other countries' coasts but not actually within their national boundaries. This is much easier than setting up an air base on land. The vast ships can hold enough supplies to refuel and rearm aircraft for missions lasting many months.

Fighter jets shoot off the flight deck and into action from an aircraft carrier.

TYPES OF AIRCRAFT CARRIERS

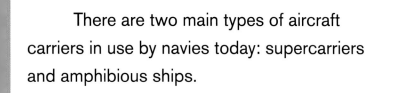

There are two main types of aircraft carriers in use by navies today: supercarriers and amphibious ships.

Very, Very Big

Supercarriers and are more than 1,000 feet (305 m) long and 250 feet (76 m) wide. They weigh around 100,000 tons (90,718 t), which is as heavy as 250 jumbo jets. This is an enormous **weight**, yet these ships are dwarfed by oil tankers and container ships that can carry four times this load.

Supercarriers generally carry thousands of crew members, more than half of whom operate and maintain the ship. The rest are aircrew members who maintain and fly the 70 to 80 aircraft on the vessel. Most of the aircraft on board supercarriers are jet airplanes. Jet airplanes need the ships' long length to reach high speeds for takeoff and to slow down to land safely. Some supercarriers also carry helicopters that can take off and land from a fixed position.

Small Carriers

Small aircraft carriers are often known as amphibious ships. They are around half to three-quarters the length of supercarriers and weigh much less. Small carriers are not quite as fast as supercarriers and travel shorter distances before they need to come to port. However, they can do things supercarriers cannot. Amphibious ships can launch quick assaults that put hundreds of **troops** on the ground. They are often used to help people after major disasters, such as earthquakes. They usually carry aircraft to support ground missions that can operate with shorter runways.

GATOR NAVY

U.S. amphibious ships are part of the amphibious force, or Gator Navy. It is so named because, like alligators, it can operate on water and land. The Gator Navy includes not only ships carrying troops on missions, but also the landing craft to get them, their tanks, and equipment ashore.

Landing craft enter and leave through the large door at the back of amphibious ships.

STEEL GIANT

An aircraft carrier may weigh thousands of tons, yet it can float very easily in water. This is a result of the **forces** acting upon the ship.

Solid Hull

An aircraft carrier's massive **hull** is the ship-shaped chunk of steel on which it floats. Steel is a very tough and slightly flexible metal. Carriers' hulls can be up to 1 foot (30 cm) thick in some parts. Inside the hull, there are incredibly strong beams running the length and width of the ship to make a strong, stable structure.

Forces

Every force in one direction has another in the opposite direction. The two main forces on a carrier are **gravity** and **upthrust**. The weight of the carrier is caused by the downward pull of gravity from the Earth on its great mass. Upthrust is the upward push on the ship from seawater below its hull. This steel giant floats because the upthrust balances out the gravity.

A giant steel carrier floats because of the balanced forces in action.

Taking Up Space

Imagine all the metal in a tanker squashed into a cube and placed on the sea. The cube has a high **density**. Its density is greater than an equivalent cube of seawater, so it would sink. The same weight of metal in the shape of a tanker hull floats because it has a much lower density than the volume of seawater that it **displaces**.

A supercarrier like this one can displace more than 100,000 tons (90,718 t) of water when fully loaded with its airplane cargo.

DOUBLE HULL

Aircraft carriers could be attacked by enemy **torpedoes** or rammed by enemy ships, so these ships have a double hull, one inside the other. If the outer hull is damaged, the inner one may remain intact. This means that seawater will not flood in and increase the ship's weight so much that the ship sinks.

HOW DO CARRIERS MOVE?

An aircraft carrier moves through the water like an average motorboat, using the push of **propellers**. Some carriers actually have four propellers, each 20 feet (6 m) wide.

Propellers in Action

Propellers have several curved blades arranged in a ring. Spinning the blades in one direction makes the curved blades push at the water they meet. Together, they produce a push at right angles. The force of water backward from the propellers creates an equal and opposite force from the water behind the ship. This pushes the carrier forward in the water. Forces that make objects move in one direction are called thrust.

A Real Drag

Carriers move forward because their thrust is greater than another force called **drag** on its hull. Drag is the backward push on the large hull caused by water rubbing against the metal surface. The larger the surface area and faster the carrier travels, the greater the drag.

The white water at the back of the ship is created by the spinning of the vast propellers.

Tugs are powerful boats that give supercarriers a push so they can maneuver around harbors before setting sail using their nuclear-powered engines.

Carrier Power

Engines produce the propellers' force. Some carriers use giant diesel engines. The diesel fuel is burned in **cylinders** in the engines to push **pistons** up and down. This movement is converted into a powerful spinning movement to twist shafts to which the propellers are attached.

Most supercarriers use steam power instead. Here, special devices, called **nuclear reactors**, are used to produce heat. The heat boils water into very hot jets of high-pressure steam. This steam power is used to spin fan blades in steam turbine engines, which move the propellers.

GOING ON AND ON

Nuclear aircraft carriers need refueling only every 15 to 20 years, whereas diesel ships need more fuel every few weeks. However, nuclear refueling can take months to complete. This is because the waste fuel is hazardous to all living things, and great care is needed when handling it.

PARTS OF A CARRIER

Aircraft carriers usually have several obvious parts built on top of the hull, but they have many more equally important parts hidden inside.

Decks

The flight deck is marked with runways. There are separate runways for takeoffs and landings. Along the edge of this deck, there are sections called **elevators**, which move up and down. They take aircraft between the flight deck and a large storage area inside the ship called the **hangar deck**.

The Island

The island takes the total height of the biggest carrier to 24 stories. Its height gives the crew uninterrupted views of incoming and outgoing aircraft, other ships, and approaching enemies. There is a good reason why this tall part is located over to one side of the ship. If it were in the middle, aircraft would risk running into it during takeoffs and landings.

Inside the Ship

There are many rooms inside an aircraft carrier. Some are where crew sleep, eat, and relax. Others are where teams work to maintain weapons, aircraft, and the ship itself. The engine rooms contain the engines that move the ship and **generate** electricity. Electricity is vital to power machines, such as the lighting system, communications equipment, and **winches** that raise and lower anchors. On giant carriers, there may also be electric **desalination plants**. Desalination plants produce drinking water for the large crew by removing salt from seawater without the need to carry freshwater.

IN BALANCE

The island, equipment, and personnel inside the ship are very heavy. This could make the ship list, or tilt to one side, and risk being unstable at sea. The solution is to build the flight deck so it overhangs the hull on the side of the ship opposite the island. This is how the ship keeps its balance.

The island towers above the hull to one side of an aircraft carrier.

ISLAND TOUR

Welcome to the island, the center of aircraft carrier operations! Starting at the top, there are many **antennae** and dishes. These are used to scan the seas for approaching enemy missiles, ships, aircraft, and submarines, and also to communicate with people on other ships and on dry land.

Pri-Fly

The top building in the island is **Primary Flight Control**, or Pri-Fly. From here, the air officer, or air boss, and his team direct all aircraft activity on the flight deck and in the air within 5 miles (8 km) of the carrier. The Pri-Fly team uses information from computers and communications equipment, and it also keeps watch through the windows found around the entire Pri-Fly deck.

RADAR

Radar antennae send out radio signals and receive reflections of the signals bouncing back from nearby objects, which could be enemies. The time taken for the reflections to arrive is used to calculate how far away the objects are.

The revolving antenna on top of the carrier is part of its radar system.

Crew on the bridge can see all around the ship from their observation windows. They have a variety of monitors and charts that help them navigate and control the ship.

The Bridge and Below

The next level down is where the commanding officer controls the aircraft carrier. This officer is responsible for the safety and operation of the ship. He issues orders to others in the team, such as the helmsman, who steers the ship, and the lee helmsman, who controls the speed of the ship. His orders also go to the quartermaster of the watch, who keeps track of the ship's location in the ocean, the direction in which the ship is heading, and whether to expect any rough sea conditions.

There are various other levels and rooms below the aircraft carrier's bridge. These include the flag bridge. From here, the admiral of a fleet, or group, of naval ships taking part in missions, including the aircraft carrier, can direct the activities of all his ships.

MEET THE CREW

A carrier crew has many jobs. Crew members always work on the same ship with the same commanding officer.

It can get pretty crowded in buildings and on the busy streets in cities, but it is even more crowded on an aircraft carrier because there are thousands of people working and living together.

Ship's Company

On a supercarrier, the **ship's company** is about 2,500 to 3,000. The company does a wide range of jobs on the carrier. There are dishwashers, bakers, specialists who look after nuclear reactors and weapons, and those who work in hospital wards.

The company is divided into several departments with different functions, including communications, deck maintenance, supplies, and safety. Within each department, there are officers and lower ranks, such as ship's mates. An additional 2,000 or so people on board live alongside the ship's company, but they are in the **air wing**. Their jobs involve operating the aircraft on board the carrier.

Cramped Quarters

Most crew members sleep in single bunks, in stacks of three, in compartments for 60 people. They each have a locker for clothes and belongings, and they share facilities including bathrooms, lounges with televisions, laundries, gyms, and canteens. The canteen on a supercarrier may serve 18,000 meals a day, but not all at the same time. Crew members move up and down between levels in the carrier using very steep steps and travel along levels through narrow corridors.

COLOR-CODED CREW

The crew members who work on the flight deck wear shirts of different colors to show what job they are doing. For example, purple crew fuel the aircraft, and red crew check its weapons. Color-coding makes deck operations safer because it is easier for the crew in the Pri-Fly and on deck to see what is happening at any time.

A yellow-shirted aircraft director uses hand signals to instruct a jet to take off.

An aircraft carrier at sea may have several aircraft on the flight deck at a time. Some are about to take off, and others are waiting their turn. Most aircraft on board are stored on the hangar deck when not in use.

Hangar Deck

The hangar deck is about two-thirds the length of the ship and around 25 feet (8 m) high. More than 60 aircraft, spare engines, and other parts are kept here. Powerful buggies push and pull aircraft around, so that they can be parked close to each other. At one end of the deck is a maintenance workshop, where aircraft are maintained and repaired. Here, the crew can fire up aircraft engines to check that they are working correctly.

Going Up and Down

Aircraft are shifted between decks using four giant electric elevators. Each of these is powerful enough to lift two aircraft with a combined weight of more than 70 tons (64 t).

This elevator has shifted an aircraft from the flight deck to the hangar deck.

Safety on Decks

On an aircraft carrier, aircraft can slide if the ship is sailing on heavy seas or when maneuvering during a battle. Crew on both decks secure aircraft to the deck using strong chains. Raising elevators to flight deck level covers the hangar deck openings so aircraft cannot fall out, even if the chains fail. Along the edges of the flight deck, there are rails and wide nets that crew members can cling to if they start to slip off the ship.

The handler and team communicate with crew on both decks to oversee movement of aircraft through the ship.

FLIGHT DECK CONTROL

Deep in the island, there is a windowless room called the flight deck control. Here, the aircraft handling officer, or handler, keeps track of the whereabouts of all aircraft on either deck. He uses a transparent model of the two decks with cut-out aircraft. A cut-out aircraft is moved to a position on the model when the real aircraft is moved.

TAKEOFF

One of the loudest, most exciting events on the flight deck of an aircraft carrier is when a jet airplane takes off.

Flight Forces

Airplanes use forces to get off the ground and into the air. They need to produce more **lift**, or upward push of air, than the downward force of gravity acting on their mass. Aircraft wings are shaped so that when air is moving fast toward them, they produce lift. At takeoff, planes angle down flaps at the back of the wings to produce extra lift.

On normal runways, airplanes speed along the ground to get air moving fast enough around their wings to lift them up. However, the runway on an aircraft carrier is shorter, so airplanes need a helping hand. This help comes from a steam-powered **catapult**. A block, called a shuttle, which is attached to the airplane, shoots forward. This flings the airplane along the runway and into the air.

Ready to Go

Before takeoff, the commander turns the ship to face the wind. This enables the moving air to help increase lift for airplanes on the runways. The blue crew moves jet airplanes to the runway, and the green crew attaches the front wheel of the airplane to the shuttle.

Then a plate rises from the deck behind the airplane. The plane's engine goes to full power. The jet of hot gases pushes backward on the plate to produce forward thrust. The pilot gives a thumbs-up, and the last crew members move out of the way for takeoff. Steam from the carrier engines shoots into cylinders underneath the deck. This pushes pistons connected to the shuttle. The airplane goes from 0 to 165 miles (266 km) per hour in just 2 seconds.

CRANIALS

Everyone working near aircraft wears a cranial. This is a light, tough helmet with a built-in visor and ear defenders to protect against injury.

Steam rises through the groove along which the shuttle moves on the runway to help airplanes take off.

LANDING

If you thought takeoff looked tricky, landing is even tougher. Imagine descending to a ship and landing a fast aircraft accurately on a narrow, 500-foot (152 m) runway.

Hooks and Wires

On normal runways, airplanes travel thousands of feet as they brake and eventually slow down. On aircraft carriers, airplanes need the help of hooks and wires. Under the airplane's tail, a metal tailhook hangs down. The pilot flies low above the deck when landing, so that the tailhook catches one of four thick wires stretched across the runway surface.

When a hook catches a wire, the wire pulls out into a V shape. A special system under the runway pulls the wire tight again in the opposite direction to the airplane. This slows the plane down from 150 miles per hour (241 km/h) to 0 in 2 seconds.

The metal tailhook produces sparks resulting from **friction** as it rubs on the flight deck before hooking a wire.

Meatball!

Pilots get help flying toward the landing strip from an optical landing system nicknamed meatball. Meatball is the name for an amber light that is part of a landing system of lights. Lenses direct red, green, and amber lights at slightly different angles into the sky. If pilots are coming in at the right angle and height, they see the meatball in line with green lights. If not, then they see the meatball out of line with the green lights or they will see red lights. They adjust their position to descend at the proper angle.

The meatball aligns with green lights so pilots know they are approaching the runway safely from the air.

TO THE SIDE

Landing runways are angled so that their ends are pointed to the side of an aircraft carrier. This is because, if airplanes miss a wire, they can take off again without crashing into the airplanes on the deck. Airplanes speed up as they are about to land, so if they miss a wire, they have enough lift under their wings to take off again and not slip over the edge of the deck into the sea.

SHIP
DEFENSES

Aircraft carriers transport their main firepower: the aircraft and weapons they carry. However, like any warship, carriers need to defend themselves from attack, especially if most of their aircraft are out on missions.

Range of Weapons

Carriers have cannons, machine guns, and missile launchers to respond to enemy aircraft that attack them. The missiles locate aircraft positions using the ship's radar systems. Many modern aircraft carriers defend themselves with rolling airframe missiles (RAMs), which are designed to seek and destroy missiles coming toward the ship. The system has sensors that detect the approach of missiles and then fire the RAMs. Once in the air, each RAM detects heat from the approaching missile and uses this to target it. The RAM collides with the enemy missile, destroying it at a safe distance from the carrier.

An RAM system can fire several missiles at once to destroy multiple threats. Each missile follows a separate target.

Underwater Defense

One threat to naval ships is torpedoes launched from submarines. Carriers reel out Nixies on long cables to defend themselves. Nixies are devices shaped like torpedoes that make loud ship propeller and engine noises. Many torpedoes hone in on noise from ships, so they aim for and destroy the Nixie instead, and the actual ship remains safe. Carriers can also launch their own special torpedoes that seek and destroy enemy torpedoes that target a ship's wake rather than its noisy engines.

If a fire breaks out on an aircraft carrier after an enemy attack, there are many fire hoses ready for action.

TOUGH SKIN

Carriers with double hulls have an extra-tough skin on certain parts of the ship. This skin is made from plates of Kevlar, which is an amazingly sturdy, light plastic also used to make bulletproof vests. Kevlar is used to protect places such as nuclear reactors, ammunition stores, and the island.

THE AIRCRAFT

Aircraft carriers support a wide range of aircraft with different shapes, sizes, and functions. These are just some of the craft on a U.S. Navy supercarrier.

Hawkeye

The Hawkeye is easy to spot because it has a large disk stuck on top. The disk houses a radar system that naval aircraft use to detect aircraft, ships, and vehicles at distances of up to 200 miles (322 km) away. This gives air forces time to anticipate attacks and to make plans to counterstrike against enemies.

Super Hornet

Super Hornet F/A-18s are the major strike aircraft of the U.S. Navy. They can shoot down enemy aircraft and carry out bomb strikes on the ground. They are shaped in ways to make it difficult for enemy radar to spot them. Super Hornets are very maneuverable and can fly at speeds of almost 1,200 miles (1,931 km) per hour.

FOLDING AIRCRAFT

Many aircraft on carriers need to have **rotors**, or wings that fold up, so they can fit on the elevators and be more closely arranged on the hangar deck.

The bombs, missiles, and ammunition for cannons are checked before each of the carrier strike aircraft's missions., such as this Super Hornet.

The wide body of the Osprey can carry many navy personnel and cargo to and from a carrier.

F35 Lightning

The F35 Lightning is one of the newest carrier aircraft. Smaller than the Super Hornet, it has similar speed but is more advanced, for example, in target identification and bombing accuracy. It is also versatile. Some Lightnings have a massive fan that can create vertical thrust. This means that they can take off and land with no need for a runway, which is ideal on shorter amphibious ships.

Sea Hawk

The Sea Hawk is a helicopter that can perform tasks including dropping bombs on submarines, rescuing crew members that have gone overboard, lifting cargo onto carriers, and flying low above ground for secret missions in enemy territory.

Osprey

The Osprey is like a cross between an airplane and a helicopter. It has a rotor at the end of each wing that can spin horizontally to lift and land, and vertically to thrust the airplane along in flight.

FUTURE AIRCRAFT CARRIERS

Today, there are approximately 30 aircraft carriers in operation around the world. Most of them are part of the U.S. Navy. Several countries will be putting new carriers into operation throughout the coming years.

Ford-Class Carriers

The new class of U.S. supercarriers will begin active duty starting in 2017. They are named after the naval veteran and former U.S. president, Gerald R. Ford. These carriers will have longer decks capable of an increased number of flights, not only of aircraft but also of flying robots called drones. They will be able to generate much more electricity than today's supercarriers. This power will be used to make the ship more automated than past carriers through increasing the amount of computer-controlled systems. It may also be used to power future laser weapons.

MAGNET POWER

The new *Ford*-class carriers feature the Electromagnetic Aircraft Launch System, which replaces steam-powered catapults. This system uses the property of magnets to repel each other, as used on **maglev** trains.

UK Supercarriers

Two new U.K. aircraft carriers are the biggest ships to ever have been used by the Royal Navy. They are due to be operational starting in 2020. These carriers have two islands: one for Pri-Fly and the other for the bridge. The flight decks have curved-up ends like a ski jump, so that Lightning jet airplanes can gain speed and use less fuel than a takeoff from a standing start.

What Is Next?

Many countries, including China and India, will soon have large aircraft carriers. Many other countries' navies will have amphibious ships. Building, maintaining, and keeping crews on carriers is becoming more and more expensive. More often today, warfare uses drones rather than aircraft because it is cheaper and less dangerous for pilots. So, in the future, there could be fewer carriers in use.

Aircraft carriers will remain an important part of the naval operations alongside other types of ship in the immediate future.

GLOSSARY

air wing Groups of pilots and aircraft maintenance specialists on a carrier.

ammunition Bullets, missiles, and other materials shot or fired at enemies.

antennae Electrical devices that send out and receive information as radio waves.

bridge The high part of a ship from which the captain and crew operate and maneuver the ship.

catapult A machine to launch an object into the air.

cylinders Closed-off tubes.

density A measure of the weight of a particular volume of a material.

desalination plants Plants that house the machinery that removes salt from seawater.

displaces Pushes aside.

drag The force of friction between a moving object and the substance, such as water, through which it moves.

elevators Electrical devices used to raise and lower weights.

flight deck The top part of an aircraft carrier used for takeoff and landing.

forces Pushes or pulls that can change the way things move.

friction The force that slows down an object when it is moving against another object or material.

generate To produce something, such as electricity.

gravity A downward force pulling any object on Earth's surface or in its atmosphere toward our planet.

hangar deck The level inside an aircraft carrier where the aircraft are stored.

hull The bottom of a boat.

island The tall part on an aircraft carrier from which the ship and flight operations are controlled.

lenses Shaped pieces of glass to bend or focus light.

lift An upward force that opposes the pull of gravity.

maglev Short for magnetic levitation, the technology that uses the push of magnets against each other to create lift and movement along tracks with reduced friction.

nuclear reactors Machines that use controlled reactions of nuclear fuel to produce heat used to operate engines.

pistons Plungers in a cylinder that move in or out when gas or liquid is forced into it.

Primary Flight Control Also known as Pri-Fly, this is the room from which crew members control the flights and movements of aircraft on a carrier.

propellers Machines with angled blades that spin to create thrust in water or air.

rotors The large propellers found on a helicopter.

ship's company Part of an aircraft carrier's crew that operates the ship.

torpedoes Missiles launched from a ship, usually from a submarine, that travel underwater.

troops Groups of soldiers.

upthrust A force, also known as buoyancy, that holds up a floating body in water.

weight The effect of gravity on the mass of an object.

winches Machines, usually electrical, to wind cable or rope in or out.

FURTHER READING

Books

Loh-Hagan, Virginia. *Aircraft Carriers*. Cherry Lake, 2017.

Nagelhout, Ryan. *Aircraft Carriers*. Gareth Stevens, 2015.

Oxlade, Chris. *Ships & Boats*. Armadillo Children's Publishing, 2015.

Websites

Due to the changing nature of Internet links, PowerKids Press has developed an online list of websites related to the subject of this book. This site is updated regularly. Please use this link to access the list: www.powerkidslinks.com/mas/aircraft

INDEX